FASCINATING
FACTS

FOR BLACK KIDS

FROM THE PUBLISHER:

THANK YOU FOR SUPPORTING A SMALL, BLACK-OWNED BUSINESS!

Please feel free to leave a review on Amazon and let me know what you think of this book. What did you enjoy? What would you like to see improved? Are there any particular topics that your child enjoyed learning about the most? I'd love to know!

Copyright © 2023 Michele Cancere.
All rights reserved.

No part of this book may be reproduced, stored in a retrieval system, or transmitted in any form or by any means, electronic, mechanical, photocopying, recording, or otherwise, without prior written permission of the copyright owner.

INTRODUCTION

In this book, you will discover fascinating facts about the contributions of black people to history, culture, and society. From inventors to scientists, athletes to artists, politicians to kings, black people have made significant impacts in all areas of life both in the modern-day and ancient world. This book even includes black culture facts from different regions of the world!

By reading this, you will gain a better understanding of the important role that black people have played in shaping our world. With various fun and engaging pieces of information, *Fascinating Facts for Black Kids* is the perfect, entertaining way for young black readers to learn more about their heritage. So, dive in and start exploring some amazing facts about black history, culture, and people!

FASCINATING FACTS FOR BLACK KIDS

DID YOU KNOW...

FASCINATING FACTS FOR BLACK KIDS

...**Brazil** has the biggest African diaspora population in the world.

The **Kingdom of Kush** was the oldest kingdom of sub-Saharan Africa. It existed from around 2000 B.C.E. to 350 C.E.

FASCINATING FACTS FOR BLACK KIDS

The **Haitian Revolution** was the only successful slave revolt in history.

African-American writer **James Baldwin** famously said, "The only way to deal with fear is to face it head on."

FASCINATING FACTS FOR BLACK KIDS

Nigeria is the biggest black country in the world by population.

Scott Joplin, a black man from the U.S., was one of the creators of ragtime music.

FASCINATING FACTS FOR BLACK KIDS

John Baxter Taylor Jr. was the first black person to win an Olympic gold medal in 1908.

The **ironing board** was invented by **Sarah Boone**, a black American woman.

FASCINATING FACTS FOR BLACK KIDS

The country **Liberia** was founded to return freed black slaves in the Americas to Africa. It means "land of freedom".

The Portugese were the first to start the **transatlantic slave trade** in the 1500s.

FASCINATING FACTS FOR BLACK KIDS

Sarah E. Goode is recorded as the first black woman to be awarded a patent. In 1885, she invented the folding cabinet bed.

Over **500** different languages are spoken in **Nigeria**.

FASCINATING FACTS FOR BLACK KIDS

In the U.S., 1-in-4 cowboys during the **Wild West** era were black.

Betty Boop was based on a black woman named **Esther Jones**. She was an American jazz singer from Harlem.

FASCINATING FACTS FOR BLACK KIDS

Botswana is the second largest producer of diamonds in the world.

African countries have the most **ethnic diversity** in the world.

FASCINATING FACTS FOR BLACK KIDS

The first black woman in space was **Mae Jemison.**

Rwanda is predicted to become the next "Singapore of Africa" (in terms of wealth).

FASCINATING FACTS FOR BLACK KIDS

Black kinky-curly hair is the **curliest** hair type that exists.

Ethiopia and Liberia are the only African countries that were never colonized.

FASCINATING FACTS FOR BLACK KIDS

African-American **Frederick McKinley Jones** was the first to successfully invent mobile refrigeration. His invention made it easier to transport food.

Black emperor **Mansa Musa** of the Mali Empire in Africa was the wealthiest man to ever live.

FASCINATING FACTS FOR BLACK KIDS

Marie Van Brittan Brown, an African-American woman, invented the first home security system.

Aliko Dangote, a Nigerian businessman, is the wealthiest black man, and the wealthiest black person in the world.

FASCINATING FACTS FOR BLACK KIDS

John Archer became the first black mayor in London in 1913.

Africans were often honored in **Ancient Greek art**, especially during the Hellenistic period between 323-31 B.C.

FASCINATING FACTS FOR BLACK KIDS

The first black **President** of the United States was Barack Obama.

The oldest human remains, called **Omo I**, were discovered in Africa.

FASCINATING FACTS FOR BLACK KIDS

The **Mali Empire** in West Africa existed from the 13th to the 16th century.

Nelson Mandela became the first black president of South Africa in 1994. He played a key role the anti-apartheid movement.

FASCINATING FACTS FOR BLACK KIDS

Oprah Winfrey, an American celebrity, is the wealthiest black woman in the world.

The quote "It is easier to build strong children than to repair broken men" is from African-American abolitionist **Frederick Douglas**.

FASCINATING FACTS FOR BLACK KIDS

Nollywood, the Nigerian film industry, is the fastest growing film industry in the world.

A 15 year old black girl named **Claudette Colvin** refused to give up her bus seat nine months before Rosa Parks did the same.

FASCINATING FACTS FOR BLACK KIDS

Bob Marley, a Jamaican singer and songwriter, is considered one of the greatest musicians of all time.

African-American **soul food** is influenced by the cuisines of West Africa and Southeastern Native Americans.

FASCINATING FACTS FOR BLACK KIDS

The Harlem Renaissance was a cultural movement of black artists and writers in the 1920s that helped define African-American culture.

Jamaican cuisine has many cultural influences, including West African, Irish, English, French, Portuguese, Spanish, Indian, Chinese, and Middle Eastern.

FASCINATING FACTS FOR BLACK KIDS

Dr. Rebecca Lee Crumpler was the first black woman to earn a medical degree in the United States.

African-American computer scientist and mathematician **Katherine Johnson** calculated trajectories for NASA's first human spaceflight.

FASCINATING FACTS FOR BLACK KIDS

Afrobeat is a style of music that originated in Nigeria in the 1960s. It's popular all over the world.

American **Ralph Bunche** was the first black person to be awarded the Nobel Peace prize.

FASCINATING FACTS FOR BLACK KIDS

The word **"hip-hop"** has its origins from the 1950s. Older people used to call house parties by teenagers "hippity hops".

Black History Month is February in the U.S. and Canada, and in the U.K. it's October.

FASCINATING FACTS FOR BLACK KIDS

African King **Kpengla** of the Kingdom of Dahomey, who ruled from 1774 to 1789, made a lot of profit from selling slaves to the British, French, and Portugese.

The Brazilian martial art **capoeira** was developed by enslaved Africans in Brazil as a form of self-defense and cultural resistance.

FASCINATING FACTS FOR BLACK KIDS

Melinda Russell's cookbook is the oldest known cookbook authored and published by a black person.

Hip-hop was created in New York City by black youth in the 1970s.

FASCINATING FACTS FOR BLACK KIDS

The **Maasai** in Kenya and Tanzania are well known for their traditional jumping dance.

Neil Degrasse Tyson is an African-American astrophysicist who has made many contributions to astronomy.

FASCINATING FACTS FOR BLACK KIDS

Chimamanda Ngozi Adichie is an internationally popular, award-winning Nigerian author. She authored the book "Half of a Yellow Sun".

African-American artist **Kehinde Wiley** is known for his paintings of Black people influenced by the style of Old Master paintings.

FASCINATING FACTS FOR BLACK KIDS

More than 2.5 million African-American men registered for the draft during **World War II**.

Desmond Tutu was a South African activist who was a prominent leader in the anti-apartheid movement.

FASCINATING FACTS FOR BLACK KIDS

African-American athlete **Jesse Owens** won four gold medals at the 1936 Olympics in Berlin.

Swahili, English, Arabic, and French are **widely spoken** in Africa.

FASCINATING FACTS FOR BLACK KIDS

The **Black Madonna** (the Virgin Mary with dark skin) is honored in many Catholic churches throughout the world, particularly in Latin America and Africa.

Ruby Bridges was the first African-American child to attend an all-white elementary school in Louisiana in 1960.

FASCINATING FACTS FOR BLACK KIDS

The first black man to serve on the U.S. Supreme Court was **Justice Thurgood Marshall**, who was appointed in 1967.

Dr. Charles Drew, a black American man, invented the blood bank.

FASCINATING FACTS FOR BLACK KIDS

In 1955, **Rosa Parks** refused to sit in the back of a bus. She sparked a bus boycott in Montgomery.

Santeria is a religion that blends West African beliefs with Catholicism. It's practiced by black people in Cuba and other parts of the Caribbean.

FASCINATING FACTS FOR BLACK KIDS

BET (Black Entertainment Television) was the first black-owned and operated TV network in the United States. It was founded in 1980.

The **1st black-owned bank** in the U.S. was the Savings Bank of the Grand Fountain United Order of True Reformers, founded in 1888.

FASCINATING FACTS FOR BLACK KIDS

The first black female **millionaire** in the United States was Madame C.J. Walker. She made her fortune selling hair care products for black women.

Jazz music was invented by black musicians in New Orleans in the early 20th century.

FASCINATING FACTS FOR BLACK KIDS

The **Ethiopian Orthodox Church** is one of the oldest Christian churches in the world. It blends Christian and African traditions.

The face of the **Sphinx of Taharqa** is based off the Sudanese King of Kush, Taharqa. He conquered Egypt and became Pharaoh in 690 B.C.E.

FASCINATING FACTS FOR BLACK KIDS

The black Pharaoh Taharqa is mentioned in the **Bible** as "Tirhakah".

Brazil was the last country in the Western Hemisphere to abolish slavery in 1888.

FASCINATING FACTS FOR BLACK KIDS

The city of **Cartagena**, Colombia, has a rich Afro-Caribbean history. Many of its people are descendants of enslaved Africans from colonial times.

The **calypso** music genre originated from blacks in Trinidad and Tobago. It was used as a form of social commentary, often addressing political and social issues.

FASCINATING FACTS FOR BLACK KIDS

Batá drums, a set of three double-headed drums, are an important part of Afro-Cuban music and religious ceremonies.

The **Zong massacre** in 1781 played a large role in the abolition of the slave trade in the British Empire.

FASCINATING FACTS FOR BLACK KIDS

The first black woman to win an Olympic gold medal for Great Britain was **Tessa Sanderson** in 1984.

Black Jamaican **Marcus Garvey** founded the Universal Negro Improvement Association (UNIA) in 1914 in New York City.

FASCINATING FACTS FOR BLACK KIDS

The **Gullah** are an ethnic group in South Carolina and Georgia who have many preserved West African traditions and their own language. They are said to sound Caribbean.

African-American U.S. Supreme Court Justice **Clarence Thomas** grew up speaking the Gullah language.

FASCINATING FACTS FOR BLACK KIDS

The **Sankofa bird** of the Akan people in Ghana represents the importance of learning from the past to build a better future.

The **1976 Soweto Uprising** in South Africa, where thousands of black students protested against the use of Afrikaans in schools, played a significant role in the downfall of apartheid.

FASCINATING FACTS FOR BLACK KIDS

The African Union, established in 2002, is an organization that promotes unity and cooperation among African countries. It works to address political and economic issues facing the continent.

The **Kente cloth**, a traditional cloth by the Asante people of Ghana, has been popularized in the U.S. as a symbol of African heritage and pride.

FASCINATING FACTS FOR BLACK KIDS

In the 1839 **Amistad** slave ship revolt, a group of enslaved Africans took control of their ship and eventually won their freedom in a U.S. court.

The **National Museum of African American History and Culture** in Washington D.C. is the only national museum in the U.S. dedicated solely to the history and culture of African Americans.

FASCINATING FACTS FOR BLACK KIDS

The **Kingdom of Aksum**, which existed in present-day Ethiopia from the 1st to 8th century C.E., was one of the most powerful states in the ancient world.

In her *Ain't I a Woman?* speech, American escaped slave **Sojourner Truth** said, "I have borne 13 children, and seen most all sold off to slavery, and when I cried out with my mother's grief, none but Jesus heard me!"

FASCINATING FACTS FOR BLACK KIDS

The **Black Panther Party**, founded in 1966 in the United States, advocated for the self-defense of black communities and was influential in the Civil Rights Movement.

Thomas Sowell is an African-American economist and writer from Harlem. He authored the book "Black Rednecks and White Liberals".

FASCINATING FACTS FOR BLACK KIDS

"He who climbs the good tree, gets a push" is a proverb from the **Akan** people - a culture in Ghana - that means choosing a good path leads to more good.

Malcolm X was an African-American religious leader and civil rights activist known for his support of Black nationalism and empowerment.

FASCINATING FACTS FOR BLACK KIDS

The **Kingdom of Aksum** played a huge role in the spread of Christianity in Africa.

In **2019**, Miss America, Miss U.S.A., Miss Teen U.S.A. and Miss Universe were all black women.

FASCINATING FACTS FOR BLACK KIDS

The **Sahara Desert** in Africa covers an area larger than the United States.

The first black footballer to play for England's national team was **Viv Anderson** in 1978.

FASCINATING FACTS FOR BLACK KIDS

The Kingdom of Kush was located in the region of present-day **Sudan**.

Sudan has more than twice as many pyramids compared to Egypt.

FASCINATING FACTS FOR BLACK KIDS

The **Kingdom of Great Zimbabwe** was a center for trading, especially for ivory and gold. It traded with places as far away as China.

Ancient Nok culture existed from about 1500 B.C.E. to 500 C.E. where present-day Nigeria is located.

FASCINATING FACTS FOR BLACK KIDS

The word **Zimbabwe** means "stone houses" in the Shona language.

In the 1500s, **Portugese** traders wrote about the Kingdom of Zimbabwe.

FASCINATING FACTS FOR BLACK KIDS

The first black president in Africa was **Seretse Khama**, president of Botswana from 1966.

Mary Eliza Mahoney was the first black registered nurse in the U.S.

FASCINATING FACTS FOR BLACK KIDS

The first African-American school principal was an educator named **Fanny Jackson Coppin**, who was born into slavery.

Carlotta Walls LaNier was the first African-American woman to walk across a stage to receive her high school diploma in 1960.

FASCINATING FACTS FOR BLACK KIDS

Okra and black-eyed peas were brought to the **Americas** by enslaved Africans.

Peanut butter has African origins. It was first created by the Azande people of West Africa.

FASCINATING FACTS FOR BLACK KIDS

Ellen Johnson Sirleaf was the first female president of Liberia. She was the first elected female head of state in Africa.

Ackee, a fruit common in Jamaican cuisine, is native to West Africa. It was brought to the Americas by enslaved Africans.

FASCINATING FACTS FOR BLACK KIDS

Moremi Ajasoro was a Yoruba queen in what is now Nigeria. She protected her people from enslavement.

Sorrel, a Caribbean drink made from the Hibiscus flower, has West African and Egyptian roots. It is enjoyed during the holiday season.

FASCINATING FACTS FOR BLACK KIDS

The **British** outlawed slavery in 1834 with the Slavery Abolition Act.

The **Nelson Mandela Foundation** works to promote social justice and human rights in South Africa and all around the world.

FASCINATING FACTS FOR BLACK KIDS

The **Mbuti** people have lived in the Ituri rainforest in the Democratic Republic of Congo for thousands of years.

The **Mardi Gras Indians** are a group of African-American cultural organizations in New Orleans. They hold parades with costumes influenced by Indigenous and African traditions.

FASCINATING FACTS FOR BLACK KIDS

Makeda, also known as the **Queen of Sheba**, is a legendary figure in Ethiopian history.
She had a diplomatic relationship with King Solomon of Israel.

Queen of Sheba is mentioned twice in the Bible, in 1 Kings 10:1-12 and 2 Chronicles 9:1-13.

FASCINATING FACTS FOR BLACK KIDS

Alice Coachman was the first black woman to win an Olympic gold medal in track and field at the age of 18.

The fastest man in the world is **Usain Bolt,** and the fastest woman in the world is **Elaine Thompson-Herah**. They are both Jamaican.

FASCINATING FACTS FOR BLACK KIDS

The **blues** music genre started in the early 20th century and is considered the foundation of many modern musical genres like rock, R&B, and jazz.

The **369th Infantry Regiment** (AKA the Harlem Hellfighters) was a predominantly black unit that fought with distinction in France in WWI, earning the nickname "Men of Bronze."

FASCINATING FACTS FOR BLACK KIDS

African American soldiers who served in **World War I** were some of the first to challenge segregation in the U.S. military. They helped pave the way for future desegregation efforts.

Motown, the record label founded by Berry Gordy in Detroit in 1959, played a significant role in the popularization of soul and R&B music in the United States.

FASCINATING FACTS FOR BLACK KIDS

Princess Sikhanyiso of Swaziland is known for her advocacy work on behalf of young people, particularly in education and HIV/AIDS awareness.

Red palm oil is a cooking oil commonly used in West African cuisine.

FASCINATING FACTS FOR BLACK KIDS

Black soldiers in **South Africa** were not allowed to fight during World War I but were used as laborers and carriers.

"Livity" is a Rastafarian concept that emphasizes living in harmony with nature, promoting a healthy and holistic lifestyle.

FASCINATING FACTS FOR BLACK KIDS

"Whining" is a popular traditional dance in the Caribbean and Africa that involves moving your hips or waist in a circle.

Gumbo is a Creole dish that originated in Louisiana, combining African, European, and Native American influences.

FASCINATING FACTS FOR BLACK KIDS

American poet **Gwendolyn Brooks** was the first black person to win a Pulitzer Prize in 1950.

Haiti was the first independent country in Latin America, and the first independent black state in the New World.

FASCINATING FACTS FOR BLACK KIDS

Jackie Robinson was the first African-American to play Major League Baseball.

Condoleezza Rice was the first black woman to serve as the U.S. Secretary of State from 2005 to 2009.

FASCINATING FACTS FOR BLACK KIDS

Reggae started in Jamaica in the 1960s and is now enjoyed all over the world.

The **Mali Empire** in West Africa was known for its gold and salt trade.

FASCINATING FACTS FOR BLACK KIDS

Jollof rice is a popular West African dish made with rice, tomatoes, and seasonings. It is referred to as the "national dish" of several African countries.

Amina of Zazzau was a legendary warrior queen of the Hausa people in what is now Nigeria. She is remembered for her military successes.

FASCINATING FACTS FOR BLACK KIDS

The Afro-Caribbean community in Panama played a significant role in the construction of the **Panama Canal**.

The music and dance traditions of the **Samba** in Brazil and the **Rumba** in Cuba have become iconic symbols of black culture around the world.

FASCINATING FACTS FOR BLACK KIDS

The **Haitian Revolution** was led by a black man named Toussaint L'Ouverture and other black leaders.

The ancient **Nok** civilization in Nigeria was one of the earliest known producers of iron tools and sculptures in sub-Saharan Africa.

FASCINATING FACTS FOR BLACK KIDS

The **Rastafari movement**, founded in Jamaica in the 1930s, is a spiritual and cultural movement that celebrates African heritage.

The **Afro-Mexican** community in Mexico has a rich cultural heritage as well as a long history of struggle against discrimination and marginalization.

FASCINATING FACTS FOR BLACK KIDS

The **Griot** tradition in West Africa involves the passing down of oral history from generation to generation through professional storytellers.

The **Black British** civil rights movement of the 1960s and 1970s aimed to address discrimination and inequality faced by black communities in the U.K.

FASCINATING FACTS FOR BLACK KIDS

The **Ashanti Empire** in present-day Ghana was a powerful and sophisticated state known for its gold wealth, artistic traditions, and complex political organization.

The **Ahmadiyya Muslim Community**, a sect of Islam founded in 1889, has a large following among black people in the Midwestern United States.

FASCINATING FACTS FOR BLACK KIDS

African-American women served in **World War I** as nurses, and some even traveled overseas to serve in the war effort.

The **Maroons** were communities of escaped slaves in the Americas.

FASCINATING FACTS FOR BLACK KIDS

During the European Renaissance, the word "**moor**" was used to described anyone with dark skin, especially blacks in Europe.

Nigerian author **Chinua Achebe** is widely regarded as one of the greatest African writers of the 20th century for his novel "Things Fall Apart".

FASCINATING FACTS FOR BLACK KIDS

George Carruthers, an African-American inventor and astrophysicist, developed the first ultraviolet camera.

Benjamin Banneker, an African-American inventor and astronomer, created the first clock entirely made of wood.

FASCINATING FACTS FOR BLACK KIDS

In many older African cultures, **hair** was viewed as a symbol of status and wealth, and elaborate hairstyles were often worn by royalty and nobility.

Marcus Garvey is credited for starting the phrase "black is beautiful".

FASCINATING FACTS FOR BLACK KIDS

In the 1970s, black actress **Cicely Tyson** popularized the **cornrow** hairstyle in the United States.

Asha Mandela holds the world record for the world's longest locs. They measure up to 110 ft (33.5 m).

FASCINATING FACTS FOR BLACK KIDS

Rastafaris believe that just like Samson in the Bible, their hair is their strength, so it should not be cut.

Alexander Miles, an African-American inventor, patented an improved elevator design in 1887 that improved safety and reliability.

FASCINATING FACTS FOR BLACK KIDS

Blacks are ranked as the most **religious** group of people in the United States.

The **British West Indies Regiment**, which included soldiers from several Caribbean islands, fought in many important battles in World War I.

FASCINATING FACTS FOR BLACK KIDS

Bria Smith, at the time a 14-year-old black student from Maryland, invented a device to detect lead in water after the Flint water crisis.

Ruby Bridges was the first African-American child to attend an all-white elementary school in Louisiana in 1960, paving the way for desegregation.

FASCINATING FACTS FOR BLACK KIDS

The 1955 **Afro-Asian Conference** in Bandung, Indonesia was a significant meeting of African and Asian leaders that aimed to promote solidarity and decolonization.

The **San** people of southern Africa have a rich cultural heritage of rock art, storytelling, and a deep connection to the natural world.

FASCINATING FACTS FOR BLACK KIDS

Some Africans were enslaved alongside Greek slaves and other enslaved people in **Ancient Greece**.

The **afro** hairstyle became popular in the 1960s and 1970s to celebrate natural black beauty.

FASCINATING FACTS FOR BLACK KIDS

Josephine Baker was a famous African-American singer, dancer and flapper girl. She was the first black woman to star in a motion picture.

One out of every three free black persons owned slaves in the **Antebellum South** in the U.S.

FASCINATING FACTS FOR BLACK KIDS

The **Antebellum Era** was the period of time after the War of 1812 and before the start of the U.S. Civil War in 1861.

Lincoln Perry was the first African-American actor to become a millionaire. He's best known for playing the character Stepin Fetchit.

FASCINATING FACTS FOR BLACK KIDS

The **Jamaican** saying "Put some clothes on your argument" means mind your words, or show some respect.

Omo Ghetto: The Saga is one of the most successful films in Nigeria.

FASCINATING FACTS FOR BLACK KIDS

Hattie McDaniel was the first black woman to sing on the radio in the U.S., and the first black woman to win an Oscar.

Sarah Forbes Bonetta was a West African princess taken captive as a child and later adopted by Queen Victoria of England.

FASCINATING FACTS FOR BLACK KIDS

A new **ocean** is forming in Africa. It started as a 60 km (37 mile) split in 2005. It grows by about 7 mm every year.

Fritz Pollard was the first black coach of the NFL, hired in 1921.

FASCINATING FACTS FOR BLACK KIDS

"Only the thing for which you have struggled will last" is a Nigerian proverb from the **Yoruba** people.

Olaudah Equiano was an African writer and abolitionist who lived in London in the late 18th century. Writing about his experiences as a slave helped abolish the slave trade in Britain.

FASCINATING FACTS FOR BLACK KIDS

In 2011, Brazil elected its first black Supreme Court justice, **Joaquim Barbosa**.

The **Palenquero language** is considered the only Spanish-based creole in the Americas that resulted from the transatlantic slave trade.

FASCINATING FACTS FOR BLACK KIDS

From the founding of the U.S. to the beginning of the 1900s, nine out of 10 blacks resided in the **South** in the U.S.

Most enslaved Africans of the **slave trade** were sent to South America and the Caribbean.

FASCINATING FACTS FOR BLACK KIDS

The **Négritude** was a movement led by black intellectuals in France. It was influenced by the Harlem Renaissance in the U.S.

W.E.B. Dubois was the first African-American to earn a PhD from Harvard University.

FASCINATING FACTS FOR BLACK KIDS

Langston Hughes was an African-American poet, novelist, and a leader of the Harlem Renaissance. He wrote "The Ways of White Folks", a 1934 collection of short stories.

African immigrants to the U.S. are mostly found in New York, Texas, California, Florida, and Illinois. As of the 2000s, around 20% live in Midwestern states.

FASCINATING FACTS FOR BLACK KIDS

Most slaves who were freed in the U.S. before the **Emancipation Proclamation** were the biracial, female children of white slave owners.

Jim Crow was the laws and customs that enforced racial segregation and discrimination in the United States following the Reconstruction period. Jim Crow lasted for about 90 years.

FASCINATING FACTS FOR BLACK KIDS

During the U.S. Civil Rights Movement,
black leaders had this saying:
"In the **South**, whites don't care how close
you get, as long as you don't get too high.
In the **North**, they don't care how high you
get, as long as you don't get too close."

The first black African to win an
Olympic gold medal was the
Ethiopian athlete **Abebe Bikila**,
who won the marathon in 1960.

FASCINATING FACTS FOR BLACK KIDS

Less than 10% of black immigrants to the U.S. from the **Caribbean** live outside of Florida and the Northeast region of the U.S.

Some slaves of Cyprus in the 16th and 17th century **Ottoman Empire** included Russians, Greeks, Croatians and black Africans.

FASCINATING FACTS FOR BLACK KIDS

American abolitionist **Harriet Tubman** escaped slavery in 1849, when she was 27 years old. She was known as the "Moses of her people".

Toni Morrison was an African-American author. She wrote the novel "Beloved" based on the true story of an enslaved African-American woman.

FASCINATING FACTS FOR BLACK KIDS

Mariama Bâ was an author from Senegal. Her book "So Long a Letter" is ranked as one of the top 100 best African books of the 20th century.

At least 12 **U.S. presidents** owned slaves. This included George Washington, Thomas Jefferson, and Andrew Jackson, among others.

FASCINATING FACTS FOR BLACK KIDS

There are a total of **54** countries in Africa.

One of the world's first universities, the **University of Timbuktu**, was founded by black Africans in the Mali Empire.

FASCINATING FACTS FOR BLACK KIDS

Third U.S. president **John Adams** stated, "Negro slavery is an evil of Colossal magnitude...It being among my first wishes to see some plan adopted, by which slavery in this country may be abolished by law."

The first black woman to win Miss Universe was **Janelle Commissiong**, who represented Trinidad and Tobago in 1977.

FASCINATING FACTS FOR BLACK KIDS

Fufu, a starchy dough made from cassava or yam, is a staple food in many parts of West and Central Africa.

In 1858, U.S. president **Abraham Lincoln** declared, "I have no purpose to introduce political and social equality between the white and the black races."

FASCINATING FACTS FOR BLACK KIDS

Pan-Africanism is the idea that peoples of the African diaspora have common interests and should be unified.

The **Three-Fifths Compromise** recognized black slaves in the U.S. as 3/5ths of a person.

FASCINATING FACTS FOR BLACK KIDS

Ethiopia is the 2nd largest African country by population.

The **Jamaican** flag is one of only two flags in the world that do not have the colors red, white, or blue.

FASCINATING FACTS FOR BLACK KIDS

The **Emanicipation Proclamation** was issued by then U.S. president Abraham Lincoln on January 1st, 1863.

Between 10 million and 12 million enslaved Africans were transported across the Atlantic to the New World in the **transatlantic slave trade**.

FASCINATING FACTS FOR BLACK KIDS

Dorothy Danridge was the first African-American woman nominated for a best actress Oscar. She was good friends with Marilyn Monroe.

The **kora**, a stringed instrument resembling a harp or lute, is a traditional instrument of West Africa.

FASCINATING FACTS FOR BLACK KIDS

NOW, A FEW QUESTIONS TO REVIEW SOME OF YOUR NEWFOUND KNOWLEDGE!

FASCINATING FACTS FOR BLACK KIDS

What's a fact about black music that you know?

Write it below!

....

....

....

FASCINATING FACTS FOR BLACK KIDS

What's a fact about black
food that you know?

Write it below!

....

....

....

FASCINATING FACTS FOR BLACK KIDS

What's a fact about a famous black woman that you know?

Write it below!

....

....

....

FASCINATING FACTS FOR BLACK KIDS

What's a fact about black
wealth that you know?

Write it below!

....

....

....

FASCINATING FACTS FOR BLACK KIDS

What's a fact about African-American culture that you know?

Write it below!

....

....

....

FASCINATING FACTS FOR BLACK KIDS

What's a fact about a black
actor that you know?

Write it below!

....

....

....

FASCINATING FACTS FOR BLACK KIDS

What's a black
saying or quote that you know?

Write it below!

....

....

....

FASCINATING FACTS FOR BLACK KIDS

What's a fact about a black latin culture that you know?

Write it below!

....

....

....

FASCINATING FACTS FOR BLACK KIDS

What's a fact about a black kingdom that you know?

Write it below!

....

....

....

FASCINATING FACTS FOR BLACK KIDS

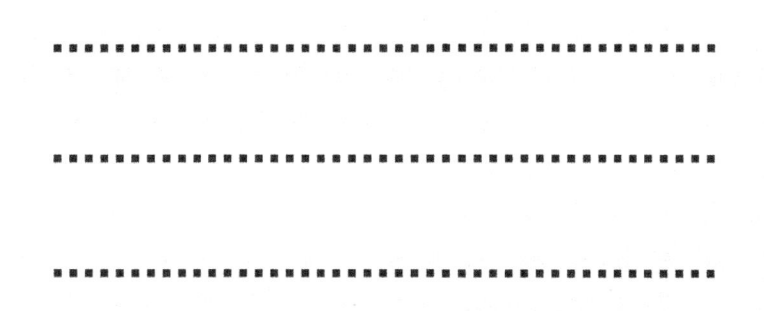

What's a fact about black
Caribbean culture that you know?

Write it below!

....

....

....

FASCINATING FACTS FOR BLACK KIDS

What's a fact about black religion that you know?

Write it below!

....

....

....

FASCINATING FACTS FOR BLACK KIDS

What's a fact about black politics that you know?

Write it below!

....

....

....

FASCINATING FACTS FOR BLACK KIDS

What's a fact about black education that you know?

Write it below!

....

....

....

FASCINATING FACTS FOR BLACK KIDS

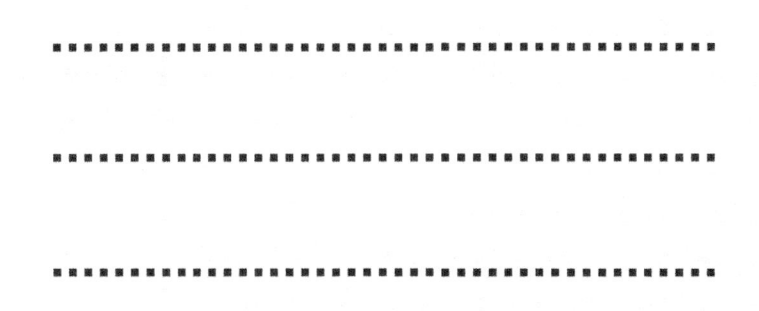

What's a fact about a black
scientist that you know?

Write it below!

....

....

....

FASCINATING FACTS FOR BLACK KIDS

What's a fact about a black writer/ author that you know?

Write it below!

....

....

....

FASCINATING FACTS FOR BLACK KIDS

What's a fact about a famous
black kid that you know?

Write it below!

....

....

....

FASCINATING FACTS FOR BLACK KIDS

What's a fact about black hair that you know?

Write it below!

....

....

....

FASCINATING FACTS FOR BLACK KIDS

What's a fact about a black invention that you know?

Write it below!

....

....

....

FASCINATING FACTS FOR BLACK KIDS

What's a fact about a famous black man that you know?

Write it below!

....

....

....

FASCINATING FACTS FOR BLACK KIDS

What's a fact about a famous foreign black person that you know?

Write it below!

....

....

....

Please feel free to leave a review by scanning the QR code below with your smartphone: